This 15 hp of 1911 has landaulette coachwork. This typical London scene demonstrates the change of function of the mews from horse and groom to automobile and chauffeur.

D0376029

THE ROVER

George Mowat-Brown

Shire Publications Ltd

CONTENTS

Published in 2009 by Shire Publications Ltd, Midland House, West Way, Botley, Oxford OX2 0PH. Copyright © 1992 by George Mowat-Brown. First published 1992; reprinted with revisions 1998; second edition 2009. Shire Library 282. ISBN 978 0 7478 0154 2.

Printed in Great Britain by Ashford Colour Press Ltd, Unit 600, Fareham Reach, Fareham Road, Gosport, Hampshire PO13 0FW.

British Library Cataloguing in Publication Data: Mowat-Brown, George. The Rover. — (Shire Album Series; No. 282). I. Title. II. Series. 629.222. ISBN 0-7478-0154-1.

Editorial Consultant: Michael E. Ware.

ACKNOWLEDGEMENTS

All illustrations, except those identified, are reproduced by courtesy of the National Motor Museum, Beaulieu. That on page 5 (lower) is from the archive of the British Motor Industry Heritage Trust, and those on pages 29 (upper), 31 and 32 are by courtesy of the Rover Group. The cover picture is from the author's collection. The author wishes to thank Daniel Young of P4 Spares and Michael Evans of the Rover Sports Register for their assistance.

Cover: *P5 P6 models from an old catalogue courtesey of James Taylor*
Below: *This 1950s view of Paignton, Devon, shows a 1935 Rover 10 hp (foreground) with a Morris 12 (left, middle ground). There is adequate space in the new car park on a busy day!*

The 1904 8 hp possessed a single-cylinder 1327 cc engine driving a three-speed sliding pinion gearbox. These, and drive to the rear axle, were contained within a tubular backbone chassis.

IN THE BEGINNING

To understand the beginnings of the Rover marque, it is profitable to look at its pre-history. In 1861 James Starley and Josiah Turner decided to utilise the skills of Coventry's watchmaking industry to found the Coventry Sewing Machine Company. In 1869 the renamed Coventry Machinists Company produced their first bicycles, affectionately called 'boneshakers'. Starley formed a partnership in 1870 with William Hillman (who was to make his own eponymous bicycles and automobiles) and engaged his nephew, John Starley, to make Ariel cycles.

John Starley and a local cycling enthusiast, William Sutton, formed a company in 1877 to make the unsteady penny-farthing type bicycles (based on James Starley's Compressus ordinaries) and safer, but expensive, tricycles. John Starley realised something psychologists would codify later: personal transport would liberate the individual's ability to rove around the country. To stress this freedom, both his 1884 tricycle and his revolutionary 1885 safety bicycle bore the insignia 'Rover'. By 1888 the company was entitled J. K. Starley and Company Limited. A contemporaneous advertisement proclaimed that 'The Rover has set the fashion to the world', and Starley experimented with a battery-powered tricycle. Rover became the company's title in 1896 — the Rover Cycle Company Limited.

After Starley's death in 1901 the new managing director, Harry Smith, decided that Rover should utilise the internal combustion engine. The first fruit was the 2¾ horsepower Imperial motorcycle of 1902; it was based on cycle principles, an area of engineering Rover understood. A year later the directors committed themselves to automobile production and recruited Edmund Lewis from Daimler.

Lewis achieved the nigh impossible; within six months a prototype had been made and Rover's first automobile, the *8 hp*, was on sale six months after that, before the end of 1904. Lewis's design differed from the accepted English practice that was a blend of Franco-Germanic automobile design and the English coachbuilding tradition. Lewis thought that the extensive use of structural timber might have been suited to being behind a horse but was not entirely satisfactory for the 'horseless' carriage! To aid confidence, the engine's compression was used to assist in stopping the car.

3

The tricycle of 1888 suffered from a familiar problem — the inability of batteries (housed in the basket) to store enough energy for the vehicle to be practicable.

The 8 hp was joined by a *6 hp* car with 780 cc engine (later, 812 cc) in 1905. A contented owner wrote to *The Autocar* in 1909: 'I have now done about 3000 miles [4800 km], and never been held up, and the only disappointment is not being able to find a hill to stop me. The car will average 20 mph [32 km/h] easily.' They were a curious pair of small cars for the birth of an automobile company, but they were produced until 1912.

The Rover Company Limited dropped motorcycles and got Lewis to design two larger cars before he left for Armstrong-Siddeley — the *10/12 hp* and the more significant 'Silent and Speedy' *16/20 hp*. The latter possessed improved suspension and a steering-column gearchange linked to a

The 4 hp New Suspended Tri-Car of 1905 was typical of the cycle-based car. These owed more to motorcycle practice than to the developing automobile.

The expensive 15 hp adopted a radiator shell that was a heart-shaped shield (as did the Rover logo — it was a common period practice for one to reflect the other).

three-speed gearbox. Power was from a side-valve 3119 cc engine that retained the 'Rover engine brake'. Its capacity would increase to 3251 cc, whilst a right-hand gearchange would operate a four-speed box for the customer with an extra £50. Two 16/20s were entered for the 1905 Isle of Man Tourist Trophy race; following some success, the cars were re-entered in 1907. The works driver, Ernest Courtis, is reputed to have been rewarded with a gold watch and an extra week's holiday for winning.

Owen Clegg joined Rover as their designer and works manager in 1910. The

This more conventional 10/12 hp was photographed in Greenwich in 1909. It was built on a wooden chassis with half-elliptic springing of the wheels. Being monoblock, its 1767 cc engine was unusual.

5

Production of all extant models ceased in 1911 for the introduction of a model that would be sold until 1924 — the new Rover 12 hp. This 1912 version is a Colonial Tourer.

Lewis-Clegg interregnum brought several variations on a theme: a 6 hp-based two-cylinder 12 hp taxi during 1908-10, and a new design, the *15 hp*, driven by a four-cylinder 2488 cc engine, for 1909-11. A pair of cars with Knight sleeve-valve engines, the counter-theme, was sold only during 1911-12. One was a single-cylinder *8 hp* of 1052 cc, the other a twin-cylinder *12 hp* of 1882 cc. Motorcycles and sidecars reappeared with a 3½ horsepower single side-valve engine of 499 cc driving the belt-driven rear wheel via an optional single or three-speed gearbox. This machine was joined later by a 5/6 horsepower twin-cylinder model. Both cycle and motorcycle

A Rover 1914 ambulance for First World War duties. The 12 hp was driven by a monoblock four-cylinder side-valve engine of 2297 cc.

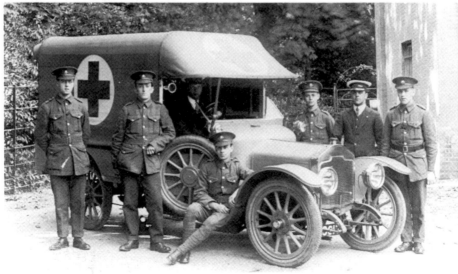

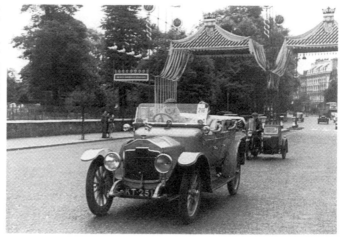

A 1914 12 hp passes Kensington Gardens on the 1953 Coronation Rally. Sales literature emphasised 'three speeds, gate change, worm-drive back axle, Bosch magneto, full inside splashers to front and back guards, and wheels made detachable'.

production ceased in 1924.

Clegg stayed for only eighteen months before joining Darracq, but he affected the fortunes of Rover for a decade. The 'Clegg' *12 hp* was based upon the sleeve-valve 12's chassis, whilst incorporating many improvements. Initially, its engine had a fixed cylinder head with integral inlet and exhaust manifolding. It was offered with various options: a four-speed gearbox; open, coachbuilt and fabric (after the style of the French builder, C. T. Weymann) bodies of two to five seats; and for those whose pocket matched their height, '6 inches [15 cm] longer ... for tall drivers'. For 1912-13, an enlarged version, the *18 hp*, was produced.

The company ceased making private vehicles between 1915 and 1919 in order to

This 1921 12 hp shows the small changes it underwent, such as tapering of the bonnet line and affixing the headlamps to the radiator. It was renamed the 14 hp in 1923.

7

A Rover 8 hp of the early 1920s by a sale notice for Eaton Grange, Cobham, Surrey, and its 'old world garden'. This curious car of 998 cc (later 1134 cc) weighed less than 8 cwt (400 kg) and could be cruised at over 40 mph (64 km/h).

A 1928 10/25 hp four-seater semi-sports of 1185 cc in an Ilkley Club Trial. It was available in saloon or sports versions with the latter attempting to rival larger and higher-priced sports cars.

This 1930 10/25 hp Sportsman's Coupé, photographed in the spring of 1931 in Finsbury Circus, London, now possessed four-wheel braking and coil ignition. A Weymann fabric body with opening roof and a luggage box were standard.

concentrate on war production. Rover supplied the British and Russian governments with motorcycles, built the 3 ton Maudslay lorry and took over production of Sunbeam's 16 hp car in staff-car and ambulance formats (allowing Sunbeam to concentrate on aero-engines). When production restarted, a small car was required to join the 12 hp. Events offered a solution: a designer, Jack Sangster, had a car with an air-cooled, horizontally opposed, twin-cylinder engine ready for production, whilst the government was disposing of a former munitions factory in Tyseley, Birmingham. Rover purchased both and the *8 hp* was ready by 1920. The cylinder heads protruded from the bonnet side panels and were reputed to glow cherry-red whilst climbing long gradients! The Rover shield (of both logo and radiator — a dummy on the 8 hp) had become squared off and the Norseman, or Viking, mascot had raised his head. The advertising men reminded owners that 'the roving spirit is in their blood' and the Rover was 'the car that set the fashion to the world'.

J. K. Starley Junior, the last of the line, became managing director in 1923. His attempts to respond to Austin's successful Seven were to bring the company near to collapse. A year before the 8 hp was dropped in 1925, its chassis was developed to accept a water-cooled four-cylinder engine of 1074 cc, the model being launched as the *9/20 hp.* (These designations took the form: taxation horsepower/estimated brake horsepower.) The 9/20 hp would progress through the *10/25 hp* of 1927, via the *Family 10* to the *Ten Special*, before replacement for 1934. In this final form, it was fitted with a freewheel, which became a Rover feature over the next two decades. The remarkable resemblance of the Ten Special to the contemporaneous Hillman Minx was due to Rover's first usage of modern steel panels from Pressed Steel, some of which were Hillman designs!

The *14/45 hp* had many distinctive features, including its automatic lubrication system and gearbox that could be overhauled *in situ*. Its four-cylinder, 2132 cc overhead-camshaft unit, with hemispheri-

9

cal combustion chambers, was enlarged to 2426 cc for the *16/50 hp* of 1926. The press was enthusiastic, and a single-seater 16/50 was entered in Brooklands Automobile Club meetings, but it was not developed sufficiently for its sporting promise to be realised.

Rover's first production six-cylinder engine, a Poppe-designed 2023 cc unit, powered the 1927 *2-Litre*, the *Meteor Sixteen* of 1933 and the *Light Six*. An enlarged version of 2565 cc gave rise to the most powerful of the range, the *Meteor*, and was used in the later *Light Twenty* and *Speed Twenty* models. The pre-1931 2-Litre and all Meteors were long-chassis vehicles, whereas the later 2-Litres and Light and Speed Twenties were on a shorter chassis; the Light Six was shorter still. In 1930, as a publicity stunt, a Light Six was used to race the 'Blue Train', the crack express, from St Raphael on the French Riviera to Calais; the Light Six won by twenty minutes. The 2-Litre was available with the usual selection of coachbuilt bodies: the *Sportsman's Coupé*, a two-door four-seater with an enormous trunk fitted at the rear, was considered particularly stylish. Another six-cylinder car appeared at the end of 1931, a

12 hp that would be known as the *Pilot*. This was a reworked 10/25 hp with a modified chassis and a Hillman-inspired six-cylinder engine of 1410 cc.

Many of the aforementioned vehicles were well enough designed and built but Britain was moving inexorably into the Depression. Manufacturers were building cars, but few people were buying them. Department stores like Whiteley's of London were attempting to attract customers with 'wonderful easy terms of payment' but these were not as 'easy' as today. The purchaser had either to pay a substantial deposit, with the balance payable over the next year, or to make 'easy payments' for a year before receiving the car! From 1927, Rover's economic state was perilous. Chairmen, managing directors and directors came and went. Spencer Wilks is credited with saving Rover from joining the long list of automobile manufacturers who did not survive the Depression. He was appointed general manager in 1929, made responsible for day-to-day running in 1931 (with his brother Maurice as chief design engineer), finally adopting the role of managing director at the start of 1933.

Left: The 14/45 hp was introduced by the Norwegian Peter Poppe. Its single overhead-camshaft engine drew most comment. This 1925 model is seen at Hampton Court Palace.

Right: A 1931 Speed Meteor 20 hp participating in the Lewes Speed Trials of 1933. A number of coachbuilders were contracted to supply the open Special bodies.

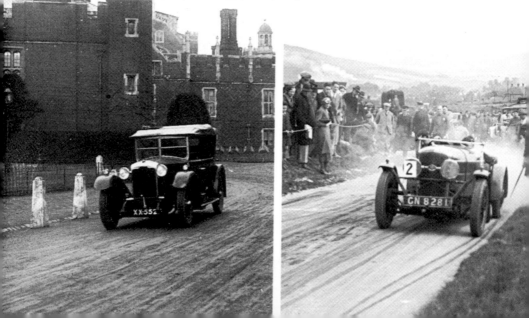

The Pilot became a 14 hp in 1932 with a 1577 cc engine — here the Fourteen Coupé of 1933. Before synchromesh gearboxes, a freewheel afforded the driver the luxury of clutchless gearchanges.

INTO AND OUT OF WAR

Production needed rationalising to return the firm to profitability, whilst the public's perception of Rover as a quality manufacturer required restoring. Following a financial crisis in 1932, the Meteor Works was sold; the New Meteor Works became the assembly plant; and Tyseley, Birmingham, produced engines and transmissions. The Pilot was uprated to 14 hp and joined by the *Speed 14 Pilot*. This latter version with triple carburettors, gas-flowed engine and low sporting body was the first of the 'Wilks cars'. The longer underslung chassis had its rear section passing under the axle; this improved interior space and suited sporting bodywork.

When a two-door coupé by Carbodies of Coventry won a coachwork award at the end of the RAC Rally in Hastings, Rover capitalised upon this. The *Hastings Coupé* was offered in Speed 14 Pilot and Speed 20 guises. The former possessed the image Spencer Wilks wanted to promote: a sporting vehicle capable of 80 mph (129 km/h)

with a modern chassis and hydraulic brakes, whilst offering above-average comfort within an aura of quality.

Germane to Wilks's idea of standardisation was a new engine with a level of commonality across the range. This three-bearing, overhead-valve unit was first used in 1933, in its 1389 cc or 1496 cc guise, to power the new *10 hp* or *12 hp* model. A year later the 12 hp and *14 hp* received the option of longer wheelbases and the range acquired Luvax-Bijur chassis lubrication. The owner-driver was not as diligent as a chauffeur in crawling under his car every week or two to attend to its lubrication requirements. It is easy to forget what 'requiring little attention' meant when *Motor* praised how reliable and easy to look after the 14 was — the engine was decarbonised only twice in the first 8000 miles (12,900 km)!

Before wind-tunnels and computer models, aerodynamics was little understood; the idea of streamlining, however, was popular. All the British railway companies were ex-

A 1935 14 hp Sports Saloon on the 1937 Welsh Rally. The bonnet still had vertical louvres, but the underslung chassis, flexible engine mounting, freewheel and chassis lubrication now extended to all models.

perimenting with it, and in 1935 Rover responded to the idea. The *Streamline Coupé* and *Saloon* were four-light and six-light respectively (referring to the total number of side windows), offered on the 14 chassis. The Coupé was also available as a *Speed 14* that was capable of 80 mph (129 km/h).

Excepting minor changes, the range continued until the new bodies for 1938 on the 12 upwards, and new engines in the *16 hp* and *20 hp*. The notchback styling continued on this body in six-light saloon and four-light sports versions. Final changes to this series for 1939 were: a new body for

The Speed Fourteen Sports Tourer of 1936, photographed in Cardiff with drivers from the Welsh Rally. They really did go rallying wearing suits and ties!

As elegant as these automobiles look today, this 1936 Streamline Saloon was perceived as being too modern by the 1930s car-buyer, and the model was dropped after two seasons.

the 10; a six-cylinder 1901 cc engine for the 14; and a new gearbox with synchromesh on the top two gears. The 10's body complemented the rest of the range whilst the new engine was a smaller version of the 16/20's six-cylinder.

As preparation for the war that seemed unavoidable, the British government instituted a 'shadow' factory scheme, siting these government funded facilities near aeroplane manufacturers. Unlike 1914, there would be ample capacity to meet road transport demands, but not that for aeroplanes. Rover joined the initial phase when

A 1938 model 12 hp saloon with updated bodywork. The most obvious differences from the earlier version are the smaller and lower headlamps, and the curvature of the front wings.

A Speed 20 at the 1937 Welsh Rally in Cardiff. The 16 hp and 20 hp were now powered by six-cylinder engines of 2147 cc and 2512 cc — refined from the four-cylinder unit.

their shadow factory at Acocks Green, Birmingham, opened in 1937. With the scheme being a success and war inevitable, Rover Shadow Factory Number 2 was started at Solihull, West Midlands, during 1939. This was to build Bristol's Hercules aero-engine.

By 1945 Rover was running six shadow and twelve dispersal factories that included requisitioned or disused cotton mills in Lancashire and Yorkshire and an underground factory near Kidderminster, Worcestershire. As well as the Hercules engine, their subcontracted work included parts of the Pegasus, Cheetah and Centaurus aero-engines, sub-assemblies of Gloster Albemarle, Lancaster and Bristol aeroplanes, aircraft magnetos and webbing for army use.

Of two projects that were to have a profound effect upon the company, the later was a direct swap with Rolls-Royce for the

earlier. In 1942-3 Rover inherited the production of the V12 Meteor and V8 Meteorite reciprocating engines (the nomenclature, being Rolls-Royce's, was a coincidence) in exchange for their classified 'top secret' work on gas-turbine aero-engines. The Meteor and Meteorite would be most famous as the power unit of the Centurion and Conqueror tanks, remaining in production until the mid 1960s.

Frank Whittle's gas turbine or jet engine was under development by Power Jets Limited in Lutterworth, Leicestershire. In 1940 the government asked Rover to assist this development, the project being relocated in Clitheroe and Barnoldswick, Lancashire. Because Whittle's engines were inefficient, Rover instituted changes and produced their B26 'straight through' version in 1942 — this became the basis of the world's first production jet engine, the Rolls-Royce Welland. Alas, Whittle rather resented

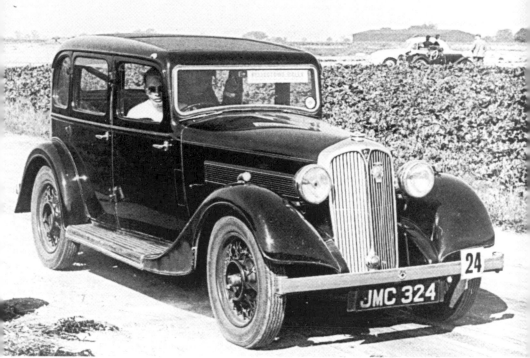

An 'old-style' 10 hp of 1938 photographed on the Felixstowe Rally of 1952. The flowing front wings would become more circular, following the tyre's shape, on the new body.

This 20 hp Sports Saloon passes the Volk's Railway on the 1939 Brighton Rally. Now standardisation was complete: one engine in five sizes, one transmission, and related chassis frames and bodies.

As exemplified by this 1946 10 hp, the post-war models were similar to those made before the Second World War, but much work was being done to design what would become the P4.

Rover's improvements. The initial letter of Barnoldswick (still part of Rolls-Royce plc) is the 'B' of engine numbers such as the RB199 of the Tornado fighter and the RB211-524G/H of the Boeing 747/767 airliners.

The devastation wrought by the air raids of the winter of 1940 on Coventry caused a reconsideration of production facilities after the war. Rover moved its main production from Helen Street, Coventry, to Solihull. Sir Stafford Cripps, the President of the Board of Trade, opened the new buildings in 1946 with exhortations to export Rover cars — the steel allocation was linked to exports. Rover, therefore, built their first left-hand-drive cars.

An interim car, the *P3* model, was ready by the start of 1948. Besides the engine, new to Rover were the frame designed by Gordon Bashford, coil-spring front suspension and an ingenious rear suspension constructed by connecting the rear of the frame

(which finished ahead of the axle) to the body with leaf springs. Old features were the transmission (with freewheel) and the general appearance: with the style of the pre-war 12's wings and bonnet, and many other panels fabricated by Pressed Steel, this was hardly surprising.

Because the artificial Royal Automobile Club horsepower rating system controlled vehicle taxation (based upon the cylinder bore diameter), manufacturers let this curious system affect the dimensions of their engines. This led to the British penchant for narrow-bore long-stroke engines. Again in the 1980s manufacturers submitted to fiscal rather than engineering disciplines, when the capacity of an engine dictated an employee's liability to personal income taxation when loaned a car by his employer (a popular incentive in commerce).

At Maurice Wilks's estate on the Welsh island of Ynys Môn (Anglesey), his Willys Jeep was rather worn out. Wilks solved his

Four-light and six-light P3s were available, with either new four- or six-cylinder overhead-inlet and side exhaust-valve engine (known as IOE) with capacities of 1595 cc and 2103 cc respectively.

The four-cylinder P3 was designated the 60, as its maximum output was 60 brake horsepower SAE and, for similar reasons, the six-cylinder became the P3 75. Here is a 1948 six-light.

personal need for agricultural transport along with the Rover problem of addressing new markets in one fell swoop — the *Land-Rover*. This was a dual-purpose vehicle that provided transport for people or livestock over rough terrain. Reminiscent of a steam traction engine, it would also, through optional power take-offs and winches, supply the motive force for such equipment as threshing machines and saw benches. The versatility of the Land-Rover led to legal battles for its lucky owners over such questions as whether it was a car, a bus or a tractor, whether it should use commercial or rationed petrol, and what the proper level of purchase tax was. Some of this litigation was not settled by the courts until the mid 1950s!

The Gordon Bashford design owed a lot to the Jeep. He even cannibalised Jeeps to save time! The Land-Rover gained an immensely strong chassis of 80-inch (203 cm) wheelbase. Power was supplied by the P3 1595 cc IOE (overhead-inlet, side exhaust-valve) engine to all wheels, permanently engaged, through two propeller shafts. The bodywork responded to two necessities: the steel shortage and lack of funds for complicated pressings. This led to a body of Birmabright alloy whose panels were simple to produce. With hindsight, this was a masterstroke; Rover's customers perceived this as a corrosion-resistant body with panels that were easy to repair. When it was released in 1948, the reception of the Land-Rover was sensational.

The Land-Rover became the standard by which other dual-purpose vehicles would be judged. This 1968 88 inch Hard-top Series 2A is in its element.

The first of the 'Auntie' Rovers, the P4 75. This 1951 example, in Cardiff on the 1952 Welsh Rally, is a late example of the 'Cyclops' front.

CHANGING TIMES

If the history of Rover is a chronicle of the aspirations and attitudes of the British middle classes, then the *P4* series can be seen as the Wilks brothers addressing the changing post-war tastes of this stratum. With recollections of the 1930s still in their minds, who could blame them? Early memories of P4s owned by the general practitioner, the bank manager or the veterinary surgeon attest to this thinking, for it was the well-heeled who could buy a new car when these expensive machines were, on the British market, made even more costly through high rates of purchase tax.

When the *P4 75* went into production in 1949, it was a brilliant response to what Rover's customers wanted. The modernist body by Maurice Wilks and Harry Loker (after the Studebaker Champion of Raymond Leowy) sported the 'full-width' style of faired-in front wings with vestigial running boards reduced to a door cill. The gentle curves and tail contributed to its flowing lines. The modernist theme extended to its rectilinear dashboard dials, column-mounted gearchange and front bench seats (all became conventional during its life). Rover realised, however, that their customers expected traditional aspects; so leather seat facings, wooden dashboard and window surrounds, thick carpeting and restrained brightwork contributed to the unmistakably British feeling of quality. When a restorer works on this series, it can be appreciated how astonishingly well made these mass-produced cars were.

The P4 75 was an extension of P3 thinking, but, as well as different body pressings from Pressed Steel (whose name seems a misnomer, the bonnet, doors and boot being fabricated from Birmabright alloy), the engine was modified with an aluminium head. Bashford also designed a new chassis, this time extending over the rear axle. This engine, a true 75 brake horsepower SAE, propelled the 75 to 82 mph (132 km/h), whilst consuming less fuel than the P3.

Developments and experiments occupied the next fifteen years. Initial changes were small; Rover replaced the 75's hydro-mechanical brakes with fully hydraulic ones and circular instruments graced the dashboard; later, the central pass-lamp disappeared. During 1950-2 an appealing two-seater sports tourer, the Marauder, made a brief appearance; it was not a Rover but used the P4's chassis and running gear — as it was designed by Spencer King, George MacKie and Peter Wilks, this was not surprising.

19

Above: *Spencer King demonstrated JET 1 on the closed Jabbeke autoroute in Belgium in 1952. He achieved a speed of 152 mph (244 km/h) — its fuel consumption being equally spectacular, at 4-6 miles per gallon (1.4-2.1 km/litre).*

Above: *A Pininfarina 75 Cabriolet at the Earl's Court Motor Show in 1953. Farina also bodied a fixed-head 90. Rover judged they would be too costly to sell in any quantity.*

Below: *Changes for 1956 raised the front wing line, offered servo-assisted braking on cars equipped with overdrive, and added two new P4s: the 105S, seen here (later 105), and 105R.*

As early as 1946, two former employees of Rolls-Royce at Derby, Frank Bell and Spencer King, started to apply their gas-turbine expertise to an idea of Maurice Wilks. Could a gas-turbine automobile engine be produced? Two problems had to be overcome: the question of scale (both size and power), and how to adapt a jet engine for road use.

In 1948 the first engine, the T5, was restricted to the test bed, but the later T8, after being tried in King's boat, was installed in a car. Bashford adapted a P4 into an open two-seater with the engine occupying the rear seat area. *XT1*, more usually referred to by its registration, JET 1, first ran in 1950. Rover was again causing the authorities some fiscal difficulty with a car running on paraffin! The world's first gas-turbine automobile is displayed at the Science Museum in London. Two other P4-based saloons followed, the *T2*, with a front-mounted engine, and the *T2A*, again mid-engined, but with an enormous exhaust funnel behind the rear window.

The engine capacity of the new *60* was 1997 cc, whilst the *90* became 2638 cc and the 75 adopted a version of the 90's. The three-car range of 60, 75 and 90 (with Laycock DeNormanville overdrive) had top speeds of 77 mph (124 km/h), 86 mph (138 km/h) and 91 mph (146 km/h) respectively, accompanied by fuel consumptions of 29 to 22 miles per gallon (10-7.8 km/litre).

A feature the owner would appreciate was the floor-mounted gear lever (which still allowed three-abreast seating), but other drivers could see his modern flashing indicators and he could see them through the wrap-around rear window, while the raised rear wings and tail allowed the luxury of extra suitcases in the boot. The *105* used twin carburettors to raise the 90's engine output, which, when tested in S form, offered a top speed of 95 mph (153 km/h). The *105R* incorporated Roverdrive, a semi-automatic two-speed transmission with overdrive.

Turbine development continued with the T3, a pretty two-seater rear-engined coupé. The four-wheel drive T3 incorporated many ideas that reappeared in production

cars, including De Dion rear suspension and inboard Dunlop disc brakes on all wheels. Amongst other modifications, the incorporation of heat exchangers improved paraffin consumption to 13 miles per gallon (4.6 km/litre).

In 1959 all existing P4s were superseded by two models, the four-cylinder 2286 cc *80* and the six-cylinder 2625 cc *100*. The 80 utilised a Land-Rover overhead-valve engine, whilst the 100 retained the side-exhaust version. These gave maximum speeds of 86 mph (138 km/h) and 92 mph (148 km/h) with consumptions of 20 miles

In 1953 Rover extended the P4 range. This was achieved by introducing a four-cylinder 60 below the 75 and the six-cylinder up-market 90, here in 1956 form, above it.

per gallon (7 km/litre). Girling disc brakes increased the driver's peace of mind when testing these. The last two models, *95* and *110*, represented the P4 range for its final two years from 1962. When *Motor* tested the 110, they found it to be the fastest P4 with a top speed of 100 mph (161 km/h), this being attributable to the attention Harry Weslake had paid to the engine's breathing, but as fuel consumption was now 18 miles per gallon (6.3 km/litre), Weslake's modifications were not that remarkable.

Spencer Wilks (left) and Donald Campbell with the first purpose-built turbine car, the T3. David Bache devised the glass-reinforced plastic body that was mounted on a box-section chassis frame.

Overlapping the P4 was the larger and in some ways more refined *P5 3-Litre*. Launched in 1958, David Bache's design contrived many superficial similarities with the P4, whilst the Rover devotee found a 2995 cc version of the IOE engine under the bonnet. The grille, side lights and headlights, front bumper, gear lever and rear lights contributed to a perception of the house style. Underneath the skin, the P5 was a more modern car of unitary construction, although the massive front subframe was related to the idea of a rudimentary chassis. Through lengthening its passenger compartment, and making it wider and lower than the P4, the P5 was made to appear as a much larger and more luxurious saloon than it was. After the Mark II saloon and coupé of 1962, detail cosmetic changes in 1966 would characterise the Mark III versions of both, until superseded by the *P5B*.

The adoption of Weslake's gas-flowed cylinder head and a lower ride-height made the 3-Litre Mark II more sporting. The saloon (background) was joined by a sleek four-door coupé.

22

This 1966 two-door coupé 2000TCZ was built by Carrozzeria Zagato on a 2000S base-unit. The 2000S was a twin-carburettor version that, like the 2000TCZ, never went into production.

MODERN METHODS AND MERGERS

Serious discussions started in 1956 on the P4's replacement, the *P6*. When Robert Boyle succeeded Maurice Wilks as chief design engineer, he was supported by Peter Bashford and the nephews of Spencer and Maurice Wilks, Spencer King and Peter Wilks. Petrol rationing was introduced following the Suez Crisis and a smaller and more economical car seemed prudent. Bright and fantastic ideas came and went, but some persisted, including the use of a base-unit, in which the floor, bulkheads, pillars and so on formed a structural whole, with everything else affixed to it. The rear suspension was a De Dion rear axle, whilst the front comprised an independent system with horizontal coils, thus allowing a wide choice of engines. All wheels had radial tyres and disc brakes. David Bache's styling department produced designs with sloping fronts (also the fashion of the Chrysler Dart and the Citroën DS); some even displayed tail-fins. The latter disappeared quickly, but it took the influence of the Wilks brothers to get, at the expense of

aerodynamic efficiency, a 'proper' nose and radiator grille.

A four-cylinder engine of 1978 cc and four-speed fully synchromesh gearbox was designed. The overhead-camshaft (OHC) engine had a flat Heron-head, with combustion chambers in the piston. Despite reservations about selling a quality car with an OHC four-cylinder engine, its efficiency made the P6 an economical large Rover: it exceeded 100 mph (161 km/h) and achieved a fuel consumption between 25 and 28 miles per gallon (about 9-10 km/litre).

Rover required a factory for the P6, but the government was restricting such facilities to 'redevelopment' areas. The compromise was planning permission for a new block at Solihull in exchange for a new factory in Pengam, Cardiff, for gearbox and axle production. As with most of these schemes, thirty years later 'Rover Way' in Cardiff led to dereliction and the need for redevelopment! The resultant delay allowed Rover to build fifteen prototypes that

23

Photographed with a 1904 8 hp, this pre-release 2000TC twin-carburettor model of 1965 had a high-compression engine that gave the car a top speed of 110 mph (177 km/h).

covered almost half a million miles.

The new managing director, William Martin-Hurst, launched the *Rover 2000* in 1963. The car was very well received by the people it was aimed at; leather was still possible for the seating and they did not mind the 'wood' being synthetic! During the P6's life, Ambla (a perforated vinyl) and brushed nylon would become the norm. It was an extremely safe motor car: so much so, the Automobile Association awarded Rover their 1965 Gold Medal for the 2000's contribution to safer motoring and Dunlop chose it as the first car to be supplied with Denovo run-flat tyres. In 1966 the range was increased to three models: the *2000TC*, *2000SC* and an automatic.

Following experiments with six- and five-cylinder engines, a larger engine arrived serendipitously. Martin-Hurst was visiting Mercury Marine in Wisconsin (part of General Motors) in 1963 when he enquired about a V8, 215 cubic-inch displacement engine that had powered cars such as the Buick Special, Oldsmobile Cutlass and Pontiac Tempest. As this 3528 cc aluminium-alloy engine (which could fit into

both the P5 and P6) was lighter and more powerful than Rover's, he obtained its manufacturing rights. By 1965 Rover were anglicising this unit under the watchful eye of Joe Turley, Buick's chief engine designer.

In 1965 J.J. Parkes, the managing director of Alvis Limited, approached Rover about Alvis becoming a subsidiary — the takeover would be to the advantage of both companies. Alvis had three ranges of products — cars, radial piston aero-engines and military vehicles — all based in a splendid factory in Holyhead Road, Coventry. The cars, the 3-litre TE and TF series, were luxurious, fast and classical, with coachwork by Park Ward Limited, but they were reaching the end of their model life and Alvis had been unable to finance the Issigonis-designed TA 175/350 replacement. The nine-cylinder Leonides and fourteen-cylinder Leonides Major engines had applications in fixed-wing aircraft, helicopters and hovercraft, whilst the six-wheel-drive military vehicles complemented Land-Rover. The benefit to Rover was both the skill and the capacity at Alvis to produce components of the V8 engine, whilst Alvis was to have benefited from two new cars based on the V8-P6. The first, the Alvis *GTS* (always known by its sobriquet of *Gladys*), was a Bache-styled three-door hatchback coupé, whilst the *P6 BS* (later called *P9*) was a three-seater mid-engined sports car capable of 140 mph (225 km/h).

By 1967 Alvis-Rover was absorbed by Leyland Motors, the controlling company of Standard-Triumph. The plan was for Triumph sports and family cars, with larger vehicles sold as Rover or Alvis. Meanwhile the 'Rover V8' was offered to the public in the *P5B 3.5 litre* saloon and coupé (the B stands for Buick). Both were automatic, as Rover did not possess a suitable manual gearbox, but this did not matter as even Bristol and Rolls-Royce sold luxury vehicles only in automatic form. The P5's life was prolonged until 1973, but this effort had been made for the potential it offered the P6.

The V8 required few changes to be made to the P6. The front crossmember had to be

The P6B 3500 (known as the Three Thousand Five), with a top speed of 117 mph (188 km/h), provided the turn of speed some customers had been clamouring for — including the police!

repositioned, the battery moved to the boot, and there was a host of detail alterations, but these were small changes considering the result. Two years after the *3500's* introduction in 1968, a North American version, the *3500S*, appeared for a season. The range also assumed its Mark II form in 1970, the obvious external identifiers being a black plastic radiator grille and structural bonnet bulges.

A police-specification Range Rover. It utilises the V8 engine, permanent four-wheel-drive, coil springs, self-levelling rear suspension and disc brakes all round. In a move that made it even more of a road car, it would later be offered with four doors and a higher level of comfort.

A merger with the sports-car maker Morgan failed, but it resulted in Morgan using Rover's V8 in their Plus Eight. With the complicity of the government, the big merger of 1968 was between the newly formed Leyland and British Motor Holdings — British Motor Corporation, Jaguar, Vanden Plas and Pressed Steel Fisher. With hindsight, it is difficult to reconcile the resultant British Leyland Motor Corporation with the contemporaneous 'big was beautiful' syndrome.

Some Rover plans continued; the King-Bashford 'luxury Land-Rover', the *Range Rover*, appeared in 1970. Its roots lay in a *Road Rover* project, but this was a new three-door (the five-door customer had to wait until 1981), boxy estate car with aluminium-alloy panelling. This was the original luxury road-going vehicle with formidable off-road capability.

A manual form of the *P6B*, curiously also named the *3500S*, had to wait until 1971. This was now a car that could be cruised at 120 mph (193 km/h) or driven in such a way as to return around 25 miles per gallon (9 km/litre). The vinyl-covered roof harmonised with the plastic grille but, if neither seems æsthetically pleasing today, they appealed enough for the roof to be an option on other models.

The treatment of the P5's replacement, the *P8*, was typical of the 'conglomerate thinking'. The large, fast and technically advanced car was cancelled in 1971 after the concomitant tooling had been ordered. BLMC had other high re-equipment costs, and Jaguar felt the P8, like the P6 BS, would dent its profitability.

Although never an inexpensive car, when production of the P6 ceased in 1976, it had sold half as many units again as all other Rover models from 1946 to the end of the P5.

One reason for the wide engine bay was the possibility of accommodating a gas-turbine engine. Rover's final saloon-car exercise in this genre was incorporated into the tenth P6 prototype, the *T4*. As it appeared in public in 1961, it predated the P6. Alvis continued development of Rover's small turbine engines until 1973, with such applications as auxiliary power units for Vulcan and Nimrod aircraft and hovercraft. The T4, P6 BS, *Rover-BRM* and the 2205 cc double overhead-camshaft engine are part of the British Motor Heritage Collection, whilst *Gladys* was retained by Bache as his private transport.

The SD1 was offered with a range of engines: the V8 and six-cylinder overhead-camshaft units of 2350 cc and 2597 cc, as the 3500 (background), 2600 (left) and 2300 (right). These were introduced in 1976, 1977 and 1978 respectively.

Above: *A new double overhead-camshaft 2205 cc engine was to update the 2000, but the 2200SC (seen here), TC and SC Auto of 1973 all used an enlarged version of the original engine.*

Above: *Some of the original P6 proposals appeared in the gas-turbine T4; it possesses the sloping front, is front-wheel drive and has swing-axle rear suspension.*

Below: *Rover's last blast of 'hot air': the gas-turbine-engined Rover-BRM sports car that raced at Le Mans in 1963 and 1965. Here it is driven by Jackie Stewart and Graham Hill in 1965.*

THE END OF THE LINE

If events following the formation of BLMC seemed focussed more on politics than products, then this would only be to presage the eventual atrophy of the once-proud Rover marque. There were a number of good new models during this end-game for British automobile mass production, but all attempts to revitalize the company proved to be false dawns.

Even by 1971, when the *Specialist Division Number One* (*SD1*) Rover model was being developed, European alternatives to Jaguar-Rover-Triumph's vehicles were appealing to adventurous customers, and Austin-Morris was especially vulnerable to Japanese imports. Despite its conventional engineering, through styling the SD1 as a large five-door hatchback of unitary construction, David Bache ensured that its size, luxury, and speed located it firmly within the Specialist, rather than the Volume Car, Division.

Although Rover was profitable, BLMC went bankrupt before the SD1 was released and the proposed related *SD2* never materialized. During Christmas 1974, the government injected large sums into the company and set up a committee under Lord Ryder, which recommended making the government the major shareholder through capital refinancing — effectively, nationalization.

Michael Edwardes, appointed chairman of British Leyland in 1977, substantially restructured Leyland cars: models were either discontinued or their assembly moved; initial links were established with Honda in 1979; and the financially important news was the expansion of Land-Rover – which now became available with a detuned V8 engine and Range Rover transmission. By the following year, all cars would be sold as Austin-Rover or Jaguar.

By 1982, the eight Leyland car-assembly plants were reduced to three: Rover was transplanted to the old Morris home of Cowley, Oxford; Austin remained in Longbridge, Birmingham; and Jaguar at Allesley, Coventry. This move coincided with the revised SD1 and the introduction of the *2000*, *Vanden Plas* luxury and *Vitesse* sports models, and the *2400 SD Turbo* with an Italian diesel engine. The SD1 acquired a reputation for poor build-quality and, alas, was never the success it had promised to be. Solihull, however, could now address long waiting lists for four-wheel-drive vehicles. The release of the Land-Rover *One-Ten*, with new chassis and coil springs, was a long-awaited modernisation – renamed the *Defender* in 1990.

The first fruit of the co-operation with Honda was the start of the *200*-series in 1984. Like most subsequent Rovers, the first digit indicates the model, the final two the engine size. The new chairman in 1986, Graham Day, renamed BL the Rover Group, the MG name being reserved for sports cars and sporting versions of the Rovers, whilst Land-Rover became the brand for four-wheel-drive vehicles. Day's background of de-nationalisation pointed to Rover's future.

The Rover *800*-series appeared in 1986, in both saloon and fastback guises. It was offered with a choice of: M16, sixteen-

The 200-series, here the 1984 model, was initially a saloon based upon the Honda Ballade and in 1989 the Concerto, but would extend to a six-model range that would last 21 years, encompass four major updates and spawn the related 400-series.

137 mph (220 km/h). The 800 range was then updated with neater bumpers, a new bonnet, and a grille reminiscent of the P4/P5, a styling theme that would be further developed as the basis of the 'retro' house style of the future models; a re-engineered 2-litre engine was also made available.

For almost two decades, everything Leyland had touched had turned to dust, whereas from the late 1980s, Rover, a subsidiary of British Aerospace (with Honda holding a 20 per cent stake and having its *Concerto* assembled by Rover), through a combination of the best British design and styling with Japanese production engineering, was re-establishing the quality of the marque in the public's mind. Rover's co-development with Honda of the *Synchro* range, and a *200/Concerto* replacement, further strengthened their collaboration. During 1992, the range was extended through the addition of diesel power, Vitesse and Cabriolet models, as well as the retrospective sports-car, the MG RV8. Alas, hindsight suggests that the woeful under-investment of this period finally set the seal for Rover's eventual demise.

The introduction of the successful *600*-series in 1993 coincided with the opening of a new facility at Cowley for the production of Rover's larger cars, including the 800-series. This was built on the old Pressed Steel Fisher factory, the majority of the Cowley site being sold off for redevelopment. The Richard Woolley-styled 600-series would eventually be made available with petrol engines varying in capacity from 1.8 to 2.3 litres, as well as turbo-charged and diesel versions. The 200/400-series was treated to a facelift that incorporated the traditional Rover grille.

After six years as a subsidiary, Rover was sold by British Aerospace to the German manufacturer BMW in 1994. As previously in Rover's history, a feeling of unease permeated both the workforce and potential purchasers

valve, double overhead-camshaft engine of 1994 cc in the *820*; a Honda V6 of 2494 cc (later, 2680 cc) in the *825/827*; and a 2.5-litre diesel. With a *Sterling* version of this series, re-badged without mention of the manufacturer, Rover briefly re-entered the North American market.

With considerable government influence, bids from Ford for the entire company (which eventually purchased Jaguar in 1990 and Land-Rover in 2000) and General Motors for Land-Rover failed, whilst British Aerospace succeeded in acquiring the Rover Group in 1988. New, or updated, models proliferated: in 1989 the Land-Rover *Discovery*, a three-door model (later also five-door) with V8 or VM turbo-diesel engine, slotted in between the Defender and the Range Rover. The 200 was replaced by a new 200/400-range in 1990 based upon the Honda *Concerto*: the former as three-door or five-door hatchbacks, the latter as four-door saloons (later also estates). The 200/400-series was available as *214/414, 216/416*, and *218* diesels and turbo-diesels. To cover the smaller-car end of the range, the Austin Metro was re-launched in Rover form with the new K-series engine, whilst at the other end, the *820 Turbo* became, in 1991, the fastest production Rover, with a top speed of

of the vehicles; this time it was accompanied by recriminations about the government's role in, and the terms of, the original sale to British Aerospace. There followed a period of acrimonious relations with Rover's former collaborator, Honda, which rapidly divested itself of its minority holding. Extensive press coverage concerning the politics of the company was relieved by the announcements of the new Range Rover, now with a 4.6-litre application of the V8 engine, and the revamped Metro, entitled the *100*.

Confidence in the company and its products started to improve during 1995 as BMW's assurances about the Rover Group seemed plausible and new products were revealed. The Woolley-styled medium-sized *400*-series, based on the Honda *Domani,* and the smaller 200-series hatchbacks materialized, as did the L-series direct-injection diesel engines. In accordance with earlier plans for the MG marque, the Rover 1.8-litre open sports car was introduced as the *MGF.* The ageing Honda V6 engine was replaced in 1996 by Rover's own KV6 – a smaller engine at 2.5 litres, but more powerful and economical.

Following an eight-year gestation, the smaller sports utility vehicle, the *Freelander,* was announced in 1997, utilizing the 1.8-litre K-series petrol and new L-series diesel engines. BMW declared its support for a coherent range of models including 'a new Mini for the new millennium'; the updating of the 200 and 400 series as the *25/45*; the further development of the K-series engines;

and the replacement for the 600/800, the 75, which was close to completion – the 100 having been dropped. Following much pre-production proving, the front-wheel-drive 75 was launched in 1999 to much critical acclaim, with four available engines: 1.8-litre, 2.0-litre and 2.5-litre V6 units, plus a 2.0-litre CDT diesel. The first cars were built at Cowley, but by the following year, the entire assembly line had moved to Longbridge.

By now, Rover was little more than a division of BMW and, with the latter's top management having departed, combined with increasing losses of £2-million per day 'not helped by the ever-strengthening Sterling exchange rate' the immediate future was cast. In 2000 BMW segmented the company and offered most of it for sale, only retaining its Swindon body-pressing plant, the new Mini model with its residual Cowley factory, and a new engine facility at Hams Hall, Warwickshire. Ford purchased the profitable Land-Rover division along with its Solihull plant, the Research & Development and British Motor Industry Heritage Centres at Gaydon, and an option to acquire the name 'Rover' if it fell into disuse.

The initial bid for the remainder of Rover came from the venture capital firm, Alchemy, led by the financier Jon Moulton. It remains unclear whether Alchemy ceased its negotiations because of a claim that BMW had not taken an active enough role with the process of 'due diligence' or whether it was

Below left: Tata Motors' Indica V2 was not an intrinsically poorly-designed car viewed as basic transport in its indigenous country, but sold at an inflated price in Europe as the CityRover with few changes other than Rover-style exterior adornments and larger wheels, which resulted in ridicule.

Below right: The Rover 600 series was produced from 1993 to 1999, the majority of the engineering being sourced from Honda. A large percentage of sales were to the fleet market.

the result of colossal opposition from national and local government, the trades' unions, and the workforce, all of whom were concerned about the effect on future employment. Phoenix Venture Holdings, a consortium of British businessmen led by former Rover chief executive John Towers, hastily assembled a successful bid and, with government approval, purchased Rover for £10, whilst receiving a dowry from BMW of £500m. The new company, trading as MG Rover Group Ltd., acquired the Powertrain engine and transmission plant at Longbridge the following year. MG Rover also unveiled the *Tourer* estate and the *MG ZT* and *ZT-T* sporting-derivative versions of the 75 to great acclaim and the *MG ZR* version of the 25.

Commentators saw the future actions of the under-funded company as a blend of fantasy and desperation. As early as 2002, MG Rover was entertaining the idea of securing a future through an alliance with Brilliance China Automotive Holdings — this foundered, as would other proposed alliances, joint ventures, partnerships, and mergers: there was even talk of moving production of the overdue replacement for the 45 to the Daewoo-FSO plant in Warsaw. The bankruptcy in 2003 of TWR, MG Rover's engineering partner, dealt a fatal blow to this much-needed replacement. The model-range was extended at each end, however. Through a product-supply agreement with Tata Motors of India, the *CityRover* attempted to address the market sector its name suggests, and through fitting the 4.6-litre V8 engine from the Ford Mustang into the 75 to produce the rear-wheel-drive *MG ZT 260*, the company had the fastest Rover since the gas-turbine days of the 1950s, with a top speed of 155 mph (249 km/h).

During 2004 it was difficult not to see the actions of Phoenix Venture Holdings as asset stripping in order to fund the continuance of MG Rover. Amongst a welter of complex financial deals: the spare-parts business was sold to Caterpillar Logistics Services of the USA; all bar 20 acres of the Longbridge site was sold to St. Modwen Properties, necessitating the company to lease-back its production facility; and the Shanghai Automotive Industry Corporation (SAIC), China's leading automaker, bought the entire intellectual rights to the 25, 75, MG TF, and the K-series engines.

Further investigation of the Polish FSO plant and a partnership with Malaysian Proton came to naught, but it was the failure of an alliance with SAIC, probably through the lack of government loan guarantees, that initiated Rover's final demise. After producing fifteen million cars, Rover collapsed on 7th April 2005 and PricewaterhouseCoopers (PwC) were appointed administrators with the unenviable task of selling what could be sold and unravelling the arcane financial structure of Phoenix Venture Holdings. Naturally, recriminations abounded that the four directors, the 'Phoenix Four', had been drawing salaries not commensurate with the company's abysmal performance.

PwC quickly realized that no-one would buy the defunct company as a going concern, so sold the Longbridge production equipment, MG name, and the engine and transmission subsidiary, Powertrain, to Nanjing Automobile (Group) Corporation one of China's oldest automobile producers. Within a year, Nanjing Automobile were exporting spare parts back to Europe, having taken a mere three months to commission the transported assembly lines, and signed a new lease for a fraction of the Longbridge site to enable the assembly of a small number of MG variants. Honda effectively prevented an afterlife for any of its joint-venture cars through reclaiming the rights and equipment for them.

As different rights to the legacy of Rover were now owned by two regional Chinese companies, the Chinese government merged SAIC with Nanjing Automobile, bringing together the former's version of the 75, the *Roewe 750* (and its related *550*), with the latter's MG versions. 'Rover' fortuitously transliterates as the Chinese characters róng (meaning grow luxuriantly, flourish, honour) and wei (impressive strength, might, power).

The option on the name 'Rover' had been exercised by Ford in 2006 and was transferred two years later to Indian ownership when Tata purchased Jaguar & Land-Rover. Not only had over a century of Rover automobile production come to an end, it also marked the demise of British-owned automobile mass production.

FURTHER READING

Alder, Trevor (compiler). A variety of reproduced road tests and other information contained within each title: *Gas Turbine Rovers 1950s/1960s, Pre-war Rovers, Rover P4 1949-56* and *1957-* (two volumes), *Rover P6 2000 & 2200* and *3500 P6* (two volumes), *Rover SD1: The Early Years (1976-7), 3500 (1977-82), 2000/2300/2600 & Diesel* (three volumes), *Rover SD1 in Motor Racing, Rover 213/216 (1984-89), Rover 800 Series 1985-1991 Including Vitesse* and *1985-1991* (two volumes). *New Rover 200 Series.* Transport Source Books, Ipswich.

Bobbitt, Malcolm. *Illustrated Story of the P4: 60-110.* Veloce, 1994.

Boddy, W. *Vintage Motor Cars.* Shire Publications, 1985.

Clarke, R.M. (compiler). A variety of reproduced road tests and other information contained within each title: *Rover P4 1949-1956* and *1955-1964* (two volumes), *Rover 3 & 3.5-litre Gold Portfolio 1958-1973, Rover 2000 & 2200 1963-1977, Rover 3500 1968-1977, Rover 3500 – Vitesse 1976-1986, Land-Rover Series 1 1948-1958, II/IIA 1958-1971* and *III 1971-1985* (three volumes), *Land-Rover Restoration Tips and Techniques, Land-Rover Discovery 1989-1994, Land-Rover 90/110 Gold Portfolio 1983-94, Land-Rover in Military Service, Range Rover Gold Portfolio 1970-1988* and *1985-1995* (two volumes). Brooklands Books, Surrey.

Dymock, Eric. *Rover, the First Ninety Years.* Dove, 1993.

Hardcastle, David. *The Rover V8 Engine.* Foulis, 1995.

Hardcastle, David. *Tuning Rover V8 Engines.* Foulis, 1993.

Hutchings, Tony. *The Land-Rover, the Early Years.* Tony Hutchings, 1986.

Long, Brian. *The Marques of Coventry.* Warwickshire Books, 1990.

Pfanmuller, M., and Schmidt, B. *Land-Rover: Dieersten 50 Jahre* (in German). Autovision Verlag, 1997.

Robson, Graham. *The Range Rover/Land-Rover.* David & Charles, 1988.

Robson, Graham. *The Rover Story.* Patrick Stephens, 1988.

Slavin, K. and J., and MacKie, G.N. *Land-Rover: The Unbeatable 4 X 4.* Foulis, 1995.

Taylor, James L. *The Classic Rovers 1934-1977.* Motor Racing Publications, 1983.

Taylor, James L. *Classic Rovers 1945-1986.* Motor Racing Publications, 1996.

Taylor, James L. *The Post-war Rover P4 & P5.* P4 Spares, 1990.

Taylor, James L. *Rover P5 & P5B: The Complete Story.* Crowood, 1997.

Taylor, James L. *Rover P6 1963-1977, 2000, 2200 & 3500.* Motor Racing Publications, 1993.

Taylor, James L. *Rover SD1 1976-86: Owners/Buyers Guide.* P4 Spares, 1991.

Taylor, James L. *Land-Rover 1948-1988.* Motor Racing Publications, 1988.

Taylor, James L. *The Range Rover.* Motor Racing Publications, 1987/93.

Young, Daniel (compiler). A variety of reproduced information contained within each title: *Advertising Rover 1904-1964* and *1904-1984* (two volumes), *Vintage Rover Anthology 1920-1933, Sporting Rover Anthology 1930-1968, Rover Anthology 1934-1949 (P1-P3), Rover Anthology P3 Scrap-book, Advertising Land-Rover Series I & II, Rover Anthology 1950-1967 (P4-P5), Rover P6 Anthology 1963-1977, Rover P6B Anthology 1968-1977.* P4 Spares, London.

PLACES TO VISIT

Bentley Motor Museum, The Pump House, Bentley Farm, Halland, Lewes, East Sussex BN8 5AF.
  Telephone: 01825 840573. Website: bentley.org.uk

Bristol Industrial Museum, Wapping Road, Bristol BS1 4RN.
  Telephone: 0117 925 1470. Closed in 2008 to be transformed into the new Museum of Bristol, due to open in 2011. Website: www.bristol-city.gov.uk/museums

British Motor Industry Heritage Trust, Banbury Road, Gaydon, Warwick CV35 0BJ.
  Telephone: 01926 641188. Website: www.heritage-motor-centre.co.uk

Glasgow Museum of Transport, 1 Bunhouse Road, Kelvin Hall, Glasgow G3 8DP.
  Telephone: 0141 287 2720. Website: www.glasgowmuseums.com

Haynes Motor Museum, Sparkford, near Yeovil, Somerset BA22 7LH.
  Telephone: 01963 440804. Website: www.haynesmotormuseum.com

Museum of British Road Transport, Millenium Place, Hales Street, Coventry CV1 1PD.
  Telephone: 024 7623 4270. Website: www.beaulieu.co.uk

National Motor Museum, John Montagu Building, Beaulieu, Brockenhurst, Hampshire SO42 7ZN.
  Telephone: 01590 612345.

Science Museum at Wroughton, Wroughton, Swindon, Wiltshire SN4 9LT.
  Telephone: 01793 846200. Website: www.sciencemuseum.org.uk/wroughton